Voluptuous Verses

Lana James

BookLeaf
Publishing
India | USA | UK

Presentation by *BookLeaf Publishing*

Web: www.bookleafpub.com

E-mail: info@bookleafpub.com

ISBN: 9789360940041

First edition 2024

D:

*Since we've met, dormant dreams rapidly
become reality... love you forever* 🤍

"Bling"

Women, listen
Tomorrow holds our freedom
But we're not prepared
Until we've shared
The knowledge that
We are all gems
Preciously gifted natural
Charms of this earth.

We have been possessed, repressed
Obsessed over
Bought and sold out
Shaped and cut down
By trivial things--
Our strength barely glistening.

We are the Diamonds in the rock
The Pearls moon mother summons from the sea.
Sapphire sister come gather
Opal, Emerald, Topaz, Ruby
Accept and appreciate individual beauty, worth
Innovate/ investigate your potential.

No longer trinkets adorning
The crowns our our kings--

We are queens.

"Brick City"

Debating dark & lovely
Versus light & white
12th grade class like a
Daytime talk show...

A sweetheart thought I might be offended,
Me-- the minority-- a New Yorker in dirty Jersey.
Hypnotized by my hazel eyes, "real" hair,
Brooklyn accent when I'm pissed...
Class Queen, (not out to himself yet), adamantly
proclaimed:
"Miss V ain't white!"

I was down, I was in.
Real knows real... every time.

Even the five pregnant students--
We read Shakespeare,
Sapphire, August Wilson, Hughes, News.
Discussed
The shots we heard outside,
How Fam around the way died...

"Chewin' the Phat"

Babe, am I a bad bitch?
Yes… and God answers prayers…

"Child-Bearing Hip"

Know what it is kid--
Been saying it longer than you
At least love isn't prejudice…
X that, it probably is, so
Plant it in a pretty pot
And call it a forest.

Take my glasses off
So I can see where I been--
Even if you drive a Beamer
Sometimes you're a pedestrian.

Downtown-- I'm the one with the tangerine colored lips
And light blue mood…
Later (or soon)

Is this train running local? There's a stop
I don't want to "Miss… do you have the time?"
No, but I'm late- I just feel it
Growing inside me like a wild tomato
((I want love))

"Cocky said, 'You ain't going nowhere' "

It was through
When she caught you
Lies
Upon
Lies
From your age
To the
Weather
And
Whether or not
You use love
Like a warm blanket
(Wanna wear it on your skin),
Just to take it away,
Get back up in it again…

"Cover Letter"

Based on my education and leadership experience
I am confident that I'm an indisputable asset
To fulfill your D's mission & vision.
I look forward to your timely response
To my advances
And welcome the opportunity
To work it in the future.

"Dessert in the Desert"

We met while I was squatting on the sand to tinkle...
Dug a hole so not to flood my open-toed soul,
Stole the last tissue from my Prada bag.

Just as my panties hit my ankles
I felt a prick on my ass.

He appeared sharp, unapproachable.
Do you want a drink? (I asked)
No thanks, I don't drink.
(Of course… always in control)

There, as I wiped, I named him "Cactus."
Arid humor left his succulent lips;
I melted into him like a drowning piece of ice.

"Epiphany"

Been
Treating
Me
Like trash yo.
Holy shittt...
Now
I
Drop
Drips!
Once
Numb
Dumb
BAM
Woke:
I'm
The
Prize,
Cash,
Medal,
Gift,
Certificate.
Had
Perfect
Attendance
In

This
"Relationship"
When
You
Just
Absent.

"Lipstick/ Make-Ups"

Her lips wore red until I said, "I'm sorry"
And suggestively listed better things than fighting.
Stress was soon replaced, with a smile,
Her lips undressed with each embrace.

I closed my eyes to kiss and wish
It's this easy next time.

"Mosquito"

Aiming to kiss voids
Holes in your souls-
Sting deep to acquire control.

Learning is burning for it.
Remember me.

Behind summer heat we fly
Sun skins say "land tonight"

Show me the best place I can bite
(You are)
Already wanting more

I'm off
On the next one...

"90s Brooklyn"

I stop to kiss my girl-
Our bodies break up the graffiti
(She's been makin love to my beeper)
Now here, I tug at her braids and stare.

She brings summer and makes me hungry
With the smooth scent of coconut
"I quit callin' you 'Boo' cuz
I don't want you ghost from my life," she said.

I smile and reassure her-
"I ain't going nowhere without you baby."
She knows to believe me.

We've had the nights of spoken dreams
Pumped with 80 oz. of the Crazy kind.
Time makes us better
And I adore calling her mine.

Her genius will supply the needy
While I become a star
We'll see the city from a tinted limousine,
Lifted from a revamped cigar.

"Until tonight"

Have to go or she'll be late for class...
Will be years before I know I'm right,
And after two kids
She still has a pornographic ass.

"Psychotropic"

Wasn't
Living
Intentionally
When you was
Together
Or took him
Back
(to back)
Back

"Rouge et Noir"

Dark piano string hair
Each strand's gloss defies humid chords.
Voice so soft in my tongue
So loud a dynasty in yours.
The way you laugh- sweet,
Petite, if I were a man
I'd have you make that sound over and over…
Sometimes bold,
You told me white is
The color of death in China.
At your wedding you'll wear
A high-necked black silk dress
With red dragon flowers.
Jade chopsticks will hold
The style of your hair
Then your groom will use them
To eat you like a snow pea…

"Slow Kiss in a Fast Whip"

{Nassau}
"Easy," she whispers.
But soon her anxious love
Can be as rough as he wants…
    So you want to come inside
    And sample every thought
    I breed of you?
    Better than omniscience— our mystery.
    Unveils slowly, as I will tonight.
    Honestly, isn't time the test this time?
    We're here…
    And we amaze each other still…

{Suffolk}
The renaissance of lust into love-
The young maiden will look away no longer
(Patience was never a virtue).
In his eyes
A challenge of depth
Or her sexiest delusion

You're everything I am, and everything I desire…

In this life they are more attractive
Then the last.
(The trees know it)
And shade them from their past.

Is it any wonder then?
When you are before me
I am after you
I always will be...

"Housewives"

I say
Women have been pimps for years.
With their
"My man"
"Baby"
"Bae"
"Zaddy"
"Boo"
"Darling"
And "Dears."
With our heels high held
Up by his ears…

I say
Women have been pimps for years.

I'm flirt, I'm fun, I'm fine.
His cards, cash stash, & ride
Now mine
Watch what you do, spend, say
Money & time

Word... we women have been pimps for years.

"Heroin"

She lies
(Especially under sheets).
She turns
And looks at this stale mate.
She lusts
And wonders when he'll give in.
But she's about to crack…

She needs
Just not more than her veins.
She tempts
To trick him into chains.
She loves—
Is even wetter when it rains.
But she's about to snap…

I can't fuckin' face you.
Don't want you to see me like this.
How am I supposed to keep you
When you vanish with a kiss?

The physical craving:
"Never again."
Telling sorrows to the floor.
(She misses so easily)
Baby, would you shake for me?
Tell me you need more.

"Manifest Destiny"

Shine.
Not like the day
When they'd expect light.
Shine.
Ripe… a grab away…
Peepshow sky tonight.

Look at you.
They will come out
And
Look at you….
Shine….

Wish come true.
You have no power
But they wish on you.
They came tonight
Just to
Look at you.
Shine.

Shooting dances in their eyes. Shoot….

Harlot or north star
Tough slut
Though bright you are…
SHINE

"Butterfly & Ladybug: Sexy Dance on a Leaf"

In obvious places waits art
Feel like I'm cheating—
Just reporting what I saw.

Hazel eyes (compare here) to fine cutlery
Have others contemplate my mysteries

Beautiful, unseasonably warm, Fall day...
Yet squirrels continue
Gathering their chill stacks

When two women make love…
Which one is supposed to call?

"Fluff & Fold"

Morning starts at 6 am.
I go downstairs and open store
Just for me.
The sign in the window say
Store hour 7 am- 7pm.
Seven days. Unless I am too too tired.
My hand grabs in the dirty white cup
Quarters hard cold like beetles.
Awake now I pour blue scented river
And feed my best machines the metal insects.
Sometimes morning early I forget gloves
And touch naked soils.

One woman "Red Bag" I call her—
Think her clothes are fancy.
I don't look, but I saw
Her panties inside yellow.
First time saw, I wash them twice.
Still yellow. And start wear my gloves.
I fold them perfect as if precious satin
And put them on red bag bottom.
Private crusty suns they become.
Sometime she give good tip for such care.

"Waaaaaaaaaaaaaaahhhhhhhhhhhhhh!!!"
Young, dark mother enter with baby and huge bag.
I didn't notice the time pass like good student.
7:38.

She has her own beetles and river.
Soon son will walk and carry their burden.
An arrogant one come and stuff in
Too much, to save a dollar.
Such greed jaded useful machines.
All his clothes are oversold famous label.

I look down at my dress of worn flowers.
No difference—
We're all just wearing laundry.

"Duh"

Four year olds' convo...

"What you gonna be when you grow up?"
"A man."

"I Dig You Baby"

It's not so easy
But is should be fun
To maintain a prize
Already won.
Kisses, caresses, love notes, support.
Honesty, trust—
Role-play for sport.

Talk to the soul.
Share, don't control.
Our actions can
Silently set a standard.

Love is not magic—
Though it may be
Luck,
Destiny,
The right time,
An earned amenity.

I dig you baby—
Like a pirate
Searching, finally unearthing
Treasure.